I0797562

Hamsters Are Fun!

Mary Elizabeth Salzmann

Consulting Editor, Diane Craig, M.A./Reading Specialist

An Imprint of Abdo Publishing
abdobooks.com

abdobooks.com

Published by Abdo Publishing, a division of ABDO, PO Box 398166, Minneapolis, Minnesota 55439.

Printed in the United States of America, North Mankato, Minnesota

052021
092021

Design: Sarah DeYoung, Mighty Media, Inc.
Production: Mighty Media, Inc.
Cover Photograph: Shutterstock
Interior Photographs: Shutterstock (all)

Library of Congress Control Number: 2019957657

Publisher's Cataloging-in-Publication Data
Names: Salzmann, Mary Elizabeth, author.
Title: Hamsters are fun! / by Mary Elizabeth Salzmann
Description: Minneapolis, Minnesota : Abdo Publishing, 2022 | Series: Pets are fun! | Includes online resources and index
Identifiers: ISBN 9781532193125 (lib. bdg.) | ISBN 9781098211769 (ebook)
Subjects: LCSH: Pets--Juvenile literature. | Rodents as pets--Juvenile literature. | Hamsters as pets—Juvenile literature. | Pets--Behavior--Juvenile literature.
Classification: DDC 636.08--dc23

SandCastle™ Level: Emerging

SandCastle™ books are created by a team of professional educators, reading specialists, and content developers around five essential components—phonemic awareness, phonics, vocabulary, text comprehension, and fluency—to assist young readers as they develop reading skills and strategies and increase their general knowledge. All books are written, reviewed, and leveled for guided reading and early reading intervention programs for use in shared, guided, and independent reading and writing activities to support a balanced approach to literacy instruction. The SandCastle™ series has four levels that correspond to early literacy development. The levels are provided to help teachers and parents select appropriate books for young readers.

EMERGING • BEGINNING • TRANSITIONAL • FLUENT

Contents

Hamsters Are Fun! 4

What Else Did You See? . . . 22

Index 23

Teacher's Guide 24

Hamsters Are Fun!

Can you find these pet hamsters in this book?

Roborovski

gray dwarf

golden

white dwarf

My pet has a blue wheel.

My pet has a red wheel.

My pet has a yellow wheel.

My pet has a pink wheel.

My pet has a green wheel.

My pet has a purple wheel.

My pet has a tan wheel.

My pet has a teal wheel.

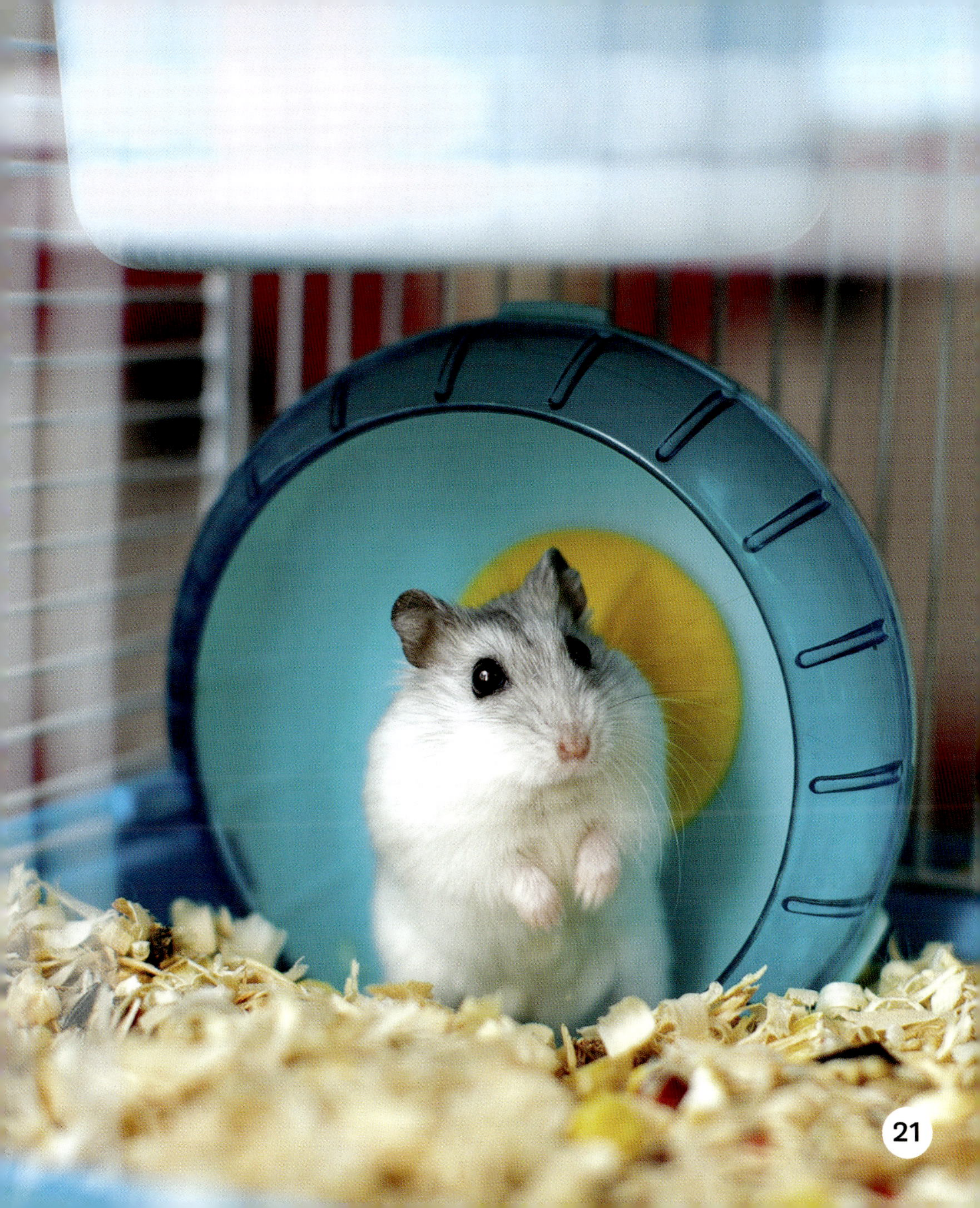

What Else Did You See?

bedding

cage

ladder

seed

Index

blue, 6

green, 14

pink, 12

purple, 16

red, 8

tan, 18

teal, 20

yellow, 10

Teacher's Guide

ATOS: 0.8 GRL: A Word Count: 48

High-Frequency Words

a blue has

my red yellow

Content Words

green, pet, pink, purple, tan, teal, wheel

Before Reading

- Tell students that the title of the book is *Hamsters Are Fun!*
- Summarize the content of the book.
- Have students look through the book. Ask them what they see in the pictures.
- Choose a few new vocabulary words. Have students predict what letter each word starts with. Then have them find the words in the book.

After Reading

Ask students questions about the book's content, such as:

- Have you ever held or petted a hamster? What was it like?
- Do you have a pet? What kind of pet is it?
- What other animals would you like to read about?